PYRAMID ROCK

JOSEPH'S JOTTER

THIS JOTTER BELONGS TO:

© Scripture Union 2005
First published 2005, reprinted 2007, PoD 2011

ISBN 978 1 84427 205 1

Scripture Union, 207–209 Queensway, Bletchley, Milton Keynes, MK2 2EB
Email: info@scriptureunion.org.uk
Website: www.scriptureunion.org.uk

Scripture Union Australia, Locked Bag 2, Central Coast Business Centre, NSW 2252, Australia
Website: www.scriptureunion.org.au

Scripture Union USA, PO Box 987, Valley Forge, PA 19482, USA
Website: www.scriptureunion.org

The selections from the book of Genesis are taken from the Contemporary English Version © American Bible Society. Anglicisations © British and Foreign Bible Soc 1996. Published by HarperCollinsPublishers and used \ kind permission.

British Library Cataloguing-in-Publication Data
A catalogue record of this book is available from the British Library.

Cover design by Kevin Wade, kwgraphicdesign
Cover illustration by Toni Goffe
Internal illustrations by Andy Robb

Scripture Union is an international Christian charity working with churches in more than 130 countries, providing resources to bring the good news about Jesu Christ to children, young people and families – and to encourage them to develop spiritually through Bible reading and prayer.

As well as our network of volunteers, staff and associates who run holidays, church-based events and school Christian groups, we produce a wide range of publications and support those who use resources through training programmes.

JOSEPH'S JOTTER

At **PYRAMID ROCK** you'll hear the exciting story of Joseph. His life went from good to bad, bad to worse and then got a lot better again! It took a long time to get better and that gave him a long time to discover that God was there with him. He had known God from when he was young. In Egypt, he learnt what it meant to really trust God.

Joseph's story is written in the first book of the Bible, called Genesis (which means 'beginnings'). To help you read the story for yourself, it's been printed in Joseph's Jotter. It's a long story, so this is a slightly shorter version. During **PYRAMID ROCK** you will not only hear Joseph's story but you'll read and talk about it in small groups. The puzzles and extra information in Joseph's Jotter help bring the story alive. Maybe you'll discover you can trust God too!

3

BEGIN AT THE BEGINNING

The book of Genesis in the Bible (the very first book) begins with God making the world! We then meet a man called Abraham. We know nothing about his life as a young man, just that one day, when he was pretty old, God spoke to him. God told him to go off on a journey and take his family with him. God said he'd show Abraham where to go and that many years later his family would be truly great! Abraham trusted God to tell the truth, so off he went! Just like that!

Many years later, one of Abraham's grandsons, called Jacob, settled down in a place called Canaan (see page 6). He had twelve sons and at least one daughter. Most of his sons got married and had children themselves. (These were Abraham's great great grandchildren — there were a lot of them!) Jacob's sons worked together looking after their father's sheep and cattle. They often quarrelled and had fights.

The eleventh son was called Joseph.

Joseph

4

WHERE JOSEPH FITTED

Joseph's family tree!

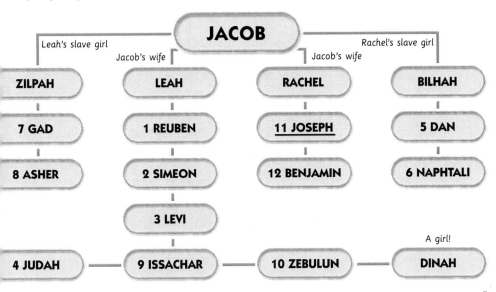

JACOB

Leah's slave girl — **ZILPAH**
Jacob's wife — **LEAH**
Jacob's wife — **RACHEL**
Rachel's slave girl — **BILHAH**

- 7 GAD
- 1 REUBEN
- 11 JOSEPH
- 5 DAN

- 8 ASHER
- 2 SIMEON
- 12 BENJAMIN
- 6 NAPHTALI

- 3 LEVI

- 4 JUDAH
- 9 ISSACHAR
- 10 ZEBULUN
- DINAH (A girl!)

CANAAN AND EGYPT

A map to help you sort out where everything happened.

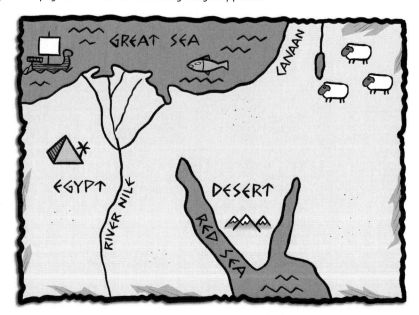

GREAT SEA

CANAAN

EGYPT

RIVER NILE

DESERT

RED SEA

6

HE ELEVENTH SON

It's bad enough having ten older brothers, but Joseph had an even bigger problem.

Jacob's two wives were sisters. Leah, the first wife, was the older sister. Rachel, the second sister, was more beautiful than Leah. Jacob loved her most of all. He also had children by the servant girls of his wives. When Jacob was an old man, Rachel had Joseph and then, in giving birth to Benjamin, the 12th son, she died. Jacob was so upset. Joseph and Benjamin were Jacob's favourite sons. Imagine what the other brothers thought of that!

 Write down words for what Joseph thought of his brothers.

 Write down words for what the brothers thought of Joseph.

Check what happened in Genesis 37:2–8 on pages 16 and 17.

7

MISSING BROTHER

Put letters in the empty squares to spell out the names of Joseph's brothers. Make sure you put the letters in the right squares! All the brothers' names are written around the side, but when you've filled in the grid you will have two names left. Who are they?

REUBEN

DAN

BENJAMIN

GAD

ZEBULUN

SIMEON

NAPHTALI

JUDAH

ASHER

LEVI

ISSACHAR

8

Answer on page

AE AND GOD'S BIG PLAN

Joseph had no idea what was going to happen to him in the future. His brothers and father had no idea what was going to happen to them. But Joseph was going to discover that God was with him in the good times and in the bad times too. This was all part of God's big plan! (Psst! Read Genesis 37:12–36 on pages 17–20 to find out just what Joseph's brothers did to him.)

GOD IS A PLANNER

aw in
e
uare
at
u look
e now.

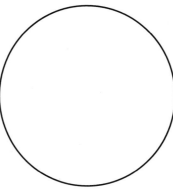

Then draw in the circle what you think you might look like in five years' time. What might you be doing?

Lord God, it is hard to think about your plan for my life, for my family and for the world. But thank you that I am part of your big plan.

9

BAD TO WORS

Joseph was taken as a slave to Egypt. His master, Potiphar, saw what a good worker he was and very soon Joseph became an important person in Potiphar's house. Read Genesis 39:1–6 on pages 20 and 21 and underline the reason why Joseph did so well.

But then things went wrong. Potiphar's wife decided she really liked Joseph. But Joseph refused to do what she wanted. So he ended up in prison. Now read Genesis 39:19–23 on page 21 and underline what the Lord God did for Joseph in prison.

Fill in the missing vowels:

L_ _RN _ N_W L_NG_ _G_

B_ _ G_ _D SL_V_

D_ TH_ R_GHT TH_NG

Psst! The Bible is split into chapters. (There are 50 in Genesis but we haven't got room for all of them.) Each chapter is then split into verses. The verse number is in small print.

Chapter 39

GENESIS 39:19–23

Read verses 19 to 23

10

OSEPH'S JOURNEY TO EGYPT

Find a route through the maze to discover what happened to Joseph in the first years of his life. Look out for the dead ends and red herrings!

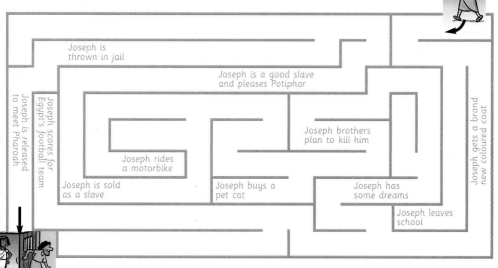

Joseph is thrown in jail

Joseph is a good slave and pleases Potiphar

Joseph scores for Egypt's football team

Joseph is released to meet Pharoah

Joseph brothers plan to kill him

Joseph gets a brand new coloured coat

Joseph rides a motorbike

Joseph is sold as a slave

Joseph buys a pet cat

Joseph has some dreams

Joseph leaves school

Answer to 'Missing brothers' on page 8 – Naphtali, Gad

11

GOD CAN CHANGE THINGS

GOD IS A **HELPER**

Imagine what it was like for Joseph!
▲ No hope of going home to his family.
▲ Unfairly thrown in prison.
▲ No hope of ever getting out of prison.
But he knew God was with him!

Write down something that you find really difficult.

Now ask God to help you cope with it. God can change things that are hard!

12

DREAMING DREAMS

In prison, God helped Joseph to interpret the dreams of the king's personal servant (cup-bearer) and his chief cook (sometimes known as a baker). Read about the personal servant's dream and what happened to him in Genesis 40:1–23 on pages 21–23.

Joseph must have hoped that the personal servant (or cup-bearer) would remember how he had interpreted the dreams. But he forgot. Two years later, the king had two dreams. No one could make

sense of them. Suddenly, the servant remembered Joseph. Joseph was called to the palace. God gave him the meaning of the king's dreams. Read Genesis 41:25–41 on pages 25–27 to find out what happened.

Joseph could never in his wildest dreams have expected this to happen!

13

JOSEPH NEVER FORGOT

Joseph was kept very busy, collecting and storing the grain for the famine which was coming. He was very successful but he did not forget his family. He was still very sad.

Read Genesis 41:50–52 on page 27. Write down the names of his two sons and the meaning of their names.

M_____ means _____

E_____ means _____

God was using Joseph to provide and care for all the hungry people in Egypt and in the countries nearby.

GOD CARES FOR PEOPLE

Choose either Joseph, the king (Pharaoh) or the people of Egypt.
Then fill in the missing words.

GOD IS A **PROVIDER**

Because God cared for Joseph/the king/the

people (cross out two of these) he provided them with

_____

Genesis 41:50–57 (see page 27) will help you fill this in.
Now fill this in for yourself:

Because God cares for _____ [your name] he

provides me with _____.

God gives us what we need but not always what we want! Thank God that he cares for you!

15

GENESIS

CHAPTER 37

[1] Jacob lived in the land of Canaan, where his father Isaac had lived, [2] and this is the story of his family.

When Jacob's son Joseph was seventeen years old, he took care of the sheep with his brothers, the sons of Bilhah and Zilpah. But he was always telling his father all sorts of bad things about his brothers.

[3] Jacob loved Joseph more than he did any of his other sons, because Joseph was born after Jacob was very old. Jacob had given Joseph a fine coat [4] to show that he was his favourite son, and so Joseph's brothers hated him and would not be friendly to him.

[5] One day, Joseph told his brothers what he had dreamed, and they hated him even more. [6] Joseph said, "Let me tell you about my dream. [7] We were out in the field, tying up bundles of wheat. Suddenly my bundle stood up, and your bundles gathered around and bowed down to it."

[8] His brothers asked, "Do you really think you are going to be king and rule over us?" Now they hated Joseph more than ever because of what he had said about his dream.

[9] Joseph later had another dream, and he told his brothers, "Listen to what else I dreamed. The sun, the moon, and eleven stars bowed down to me."

[10] When he told his father about this dream, his father became angry and said, "What's that supposed to mean? Are your mother and I and your brothers all going to come and bow down in front of you?" 11 Joseph's brothers were jealous of him, but his father kept wondering about the dream.

[12] One day when Joseph's brothers had taken the sheep to a pasture near Shechem, [13] his father Jacob said to him, "I want you to go to your brothers. They are with the sheep near Shechem."

"Yes, sir," Joseph answered.

[14] His father said, "Go and find out how your brothers and the sheep are doing. Then come back and let me know." So he sent him from Hebron Valley.

Joseph was near Shechem [15] and wandering through the fields, when a man asked, "What are you looking for?"

[16] Joseph answered, "I'm looking for my brothers who are watching the sheep. Can you tell me where they are?"

[17] "They're not here any more," the man replied. "I overheard them say they were going to Dothan."

Joseph left and found his brothers in Dothan. [18] But before he got there, they saw him coming and made plans to kill him. [19] They said to one another, "Look, here comes the hero of those dreams! [20] Let's kill him and throw him into a pit and say that some wild animal ate him. Then we'll see what happens to those dreams."

[21] Reuben heard this and tried to protect Joseph from them. "Let's not kill him," he said. [22] "Don't murder him or even harm him. Just throw him into a dry well out here in the desert." Reuben planned to rescue Joseph later and take him back to his father.

[23] When Joseph came to his brothers, they pulled off his fine coat [24] and

threw him into a dry well.

25 As Joseph's brothers sat down to eat, they looked up and saw a caravan of Ishmaelites coming from Gilead. Their camels were loaded with all kinds of spices that they were taking to Egypt. 26 So Judah said, "What will we gain if we kill our brother and hide his body? 27 Let's sell him to the Ishmaelites and not harm him. After all, he is our brother." And the others agreed.

28 When the Midianite merchants came by, Joseph's brothers took him out of the well, and for twenty pieces of silver they sold him to the Ishmaelites who took him to Egypt.

29 When Reuben returned to the well and did not find Joseph there, he tore his clothes in sorrow. 30 Then he went back to his brothers and said, "The boy is gone! What am I going to do?"

31 Joseph's brothers killed a goat and dipped Joseph's fine coat in its blood. 32 After this, they took the coat to their father and said, "We found this! Look at it carefully and see if it belongs to your son."

33 Jacob knew it was Joseph's coat and said, "It's my son's coat! Joseph

has been torn to pieces and eaten by some wild animal."

[34] Jacob mourned for Joseph a long time, and to show his sorrow he tore his clothes and wore sackcloth. [35] All Jacob's children came to comfort him, but he refused to be comforted. "No," he said, "I will go to my grave, mourning for my son." So Jacob kept on grieving.

[36] Meanwhile, the Midianites had sold Joseph in Egypt to a man named Potiphar, who was the king's official in charge of the palace guard.

CHAPTER 39

[1] The Ishmaelites took Joseph to Egypt and sold him to Potiphar, the king's official in charge of the palace guard. [2-3] So Joseph lived in the home of Potiphar, his Egyptian owner.

Soon Potiphar realized that the Lord was helping Joseph to be successful in whatever he did. [4] Potiphar liked Joseph and made him his personal assistant, putting him in charge of his house and all his property. [5] Because of Joseph, the Lord began to bless Potiphar's family and fields. [6] Potiphar left everything up to

Joseph, and with Joseph there, the only decision he had to make was what he wanted to eat. Joseph was well-built and handsome,

19 Potiphar became very angry 20 and threw Joseph in the same prison where the king's prisoners were kept.

While Joseph was in prison, 21 the Lord helped him and was good to him. He even made the jailer like Joseph so much that 22 he put him in charge of the other prisoners and of everything that was done in the jail. 23 The jailer did not worry about anything, because the Lord was with Joseph and made him successful in all that he did.

CHAPTER 40

1–3 While Joseph was in prison, both the king's personal servant and his chief cook made the king angry. So he had them thrown into the same prison with Joseph. 4 They spent a long time in prison, and Potiphar, the official in charge of the palace guard, made Joseph their servant.

[5] One night each of the two men had a dream, but their dreams had different meanings. [6] The next morning, when Joseph went to see the men, he could tell they were upset, [7] and he asked, "Why are you so worried today?"

[8] "We each had a dream last night," they answered, "and there is no one to tell us what they mean."

Joseph replied, "Doesn't God know the meaning of dreams? Now tell me what you dreamed."

[9] The king's personal servant told Joseph, "In my dream I saw a vine [10] with three branches. As soon as it budded, it blossomed, and its grapes became ripe. [11] I held the king's cup and squeezed the grapes into it, then I gave the cup to the king."

[12] Joseph said:

This is the meaning of your dream. The three branches stand for three days, [13] and in three days the king will pardon you. He will make you his personal servant again, and you will serve him his wine, just as you used to do. [14] But when these good things happen, please don't forget to tell the king about me, so I can get out of this place. [15] I was kidnapped from the land of the Hebrews, and here in Egypt I haven't done anything to deserve being thrown in jail.

[22] Everything happened just as Joseph had said it would, [23] but the king's personal servant completely forgot about Joseph.

CHAPTER 41

[1] Two years later the king of Egypt dreamed he was standing beside the River Nile. [2] Suddenly, seven fat, healthy cows came up from the river and started eating grass along the bank. [3] Then seven ugly, skinny cows came up out of the river and [4] ate the fat, healthy cows. When this happened, the king woke up.

[5] The king went back to sleep and had another dream. This time seven full heads of grain were growing on a single stalk. [6] Later, seven other heads of grain appeared, but they were thin and scorched by the east wind. [7] The thin heads of grain swallowed the seven full heads. Again the king woke up, and it

had only been a dream.

8 The next morning the king was upset. So he called in his magicians and wise men and told them what he had dreamed. None of them could tell him what the dreams meant.

9 The king's personal servant said:

Now I remember what I was supposed to do. 10 When you were angry with me and your chief cook, you threw us both in jail in the house of the captain of the guard. 11 One night we both had dreams, and each dream had a different meaning. 12 A young Hebrew, who was a servant of the captain of the guard, was there with us at the time. When we told him our dreams, he explained what each of them meant, 13 and everything happened just as he said it would. I got my job back, and the cook was put to death.

14 The king sent for Joseph, who was quickly brought out of jail. He shaved, changed his clothes, and went to the king.

[15] The king said to him, "I had a dream, yet no one can explain what it means. I am told that you can interpret dreams."

[16] "Your Majesty," Joseph answered, "I can't do it myself, but God can give a good meaning to your dreams."

[25] Joseph replied:

Your Majesty, both of your dreams mean the same thing, and in them God has shown what he is going to do. [26] The seven good cows stand for seven years, and so do the seven good heads of grain. [27] The seven skinny, ugly cows that came up later also stand for seven years, as do the seven bad heads of grain that were scorched by the east wind. The dreams mean there will be seven years when there won't be enough grain.

[28] It is just as I said—God has shown what he intends to do. [29] For seven years Egypt will have more than enough grain, [30] but that will be followed by seven years when there won't be enough. The good years of plenty will be forgotten, and everywhere in Egypt people will be starving.

[31] The famine will be so bad that no one will remember that once there had been plenty. [32] God has given you two dreams to let you know that he has definitely decided to do this and that he will do it soon.

[33] Your Majesty, you should find someone who is wise and will know what to do, so that you can put him in charge of all Egypt. [34] Then appoint some other officials to collect one-fifth of every crop harvested in Egypt during the seven years when there is plenty. [35] Give them the power to collect the grain during those good years and to store it in your cities. [36] It can be stored until it is needed during the seven years when there won't be enough grain in Egypt. This will keep the country from being destroyed because of the lack of food.

[37] The king and his officials liked this plan. [38] So the king said to them, "No one could possibly handle this better than Joseph, since the Spirit of God is with him."

[39] The king told Joseph, "God is the one who has shown you these things.

No one else is as wise as you are or knows as much as you do. 40 I'm putting you in charge of my palace, and everybody will have to obey you. No one will be over you except me. 41 You are now governor of all Egypt!"

50 Joseph and his wife had two sons before the famine began. 51 Their first son was named Manasseh, which means, "God has let me forget all my troubles and my family back home." 52 His second son was named Ephraim, which means "God has made me a success in the land where I suffered."
53 Egypt's seven years of plenty came to an end, 54 and the seven years of famine began, just as Joseph had said. There was not enough food in other countries, but all over Egypt there was plenty. 55 When the famine finally struck Egypt, the people asked the king for food, but he said, "Go to Joseph and do what he tells you to do."
56 The famine became bad everywhere in Egypt, so Joseph opened the storehouses and sold the grain to the Egyptians. 57 People from all over the world came to Egypt, because the famine was severe in their countries.

CHAPTER 43

[1] The famine in Canaan got worse, [2] until finally, Jacob's family had eaten all the grain they had bought in Egypt. So Jacob said to his sons, "Go back and buy some more grain."

[3-5] Judah replied, "The governor strictly warned us that we would not be allowed to see him unless we brought our youngest brother with us. If you let us take Benjamin along, we will go and buy grain. But we won't go without him!"

[6] Jacob asked, "Why did you cause me so much trouble by telling the governor you had another brother?"

[7] They answered, "He asked a lot of questions about us and our family. He wanted to know if you were still alive and if we had any more brothers. All we could do was answer his questions. How could we know he would tell us to bring along our brother?"

[15] The brothers took the gifts, twice the amount of money, and Benjamin.

Then they hurried off to Egypt. When they stood in front of Joseph, [16] he saw Benjamin and told the servant in charge of his house, "Take these men to my house. Slaughter an animal and cook it, so they can eat with me at midday." [32] Joseph was served at a table by himself, and his brothers were served at another. The Egyptians sat at yet another table, because Egyptians felt it was disgusting to eat with Hebrews. [33] To the surprise of Joseph's brothers, they were seated in front of him according to their ages, from the eldest to the youngest. [34] They were served food from Joseph's table, and Benjamin was given five times as much as each of the others. So Joseph's brothers drank with him and had a good time.

CHAPTER 44

[1-2] Later, Joseph told the servant in charge of his house, "Fill the men's grain sacks with as much as they can hold and put their money in the sacks. Also put my silver cup in the sack of the youngest brother." The servant did as he was told.

[3] Early the next morning, the men were sent on their way with their donkeys. [4] But they had not gone far from the city when Joseph told the servant, "Go after those men! When you catch them, say, 'My master has been good to you. So why have you stolen his silver cup? [5] Not only does he drink from his cup, but he also uses it to learn about the future. You have done a terrible thing.'"

[6] When the servant caught up with them, he said exactly what Joseph had told him to say. [7] But they replied, "Sir, why do you say such things? We would never do anything like that! [8] We even returned the money we found in our grain sacks when we got back to Canaan. So why would we want to steal any silver or gold from your master's house? [9] If you find that one of us has the cup, then kill him, and the rest of us will become your slaves."

[10] "Good!" the man replied, "I'll do what you have said. But only the one who has the cup will become my slave. The rest of you can go free."

[11] Each of the brothers quickly put his sack on the ground and opened it. [12] Joseph's servant started searching the sacks, beginning with the one that

belonged to the eldest brother. When he came to Benjamin's sack, he found the cup. 13 This upset the brothers so much that they began tearing their clothes in sorrow. Then they loaded their donkeys and returned to the city.

14 When Judah and his brothers got there, Joseph was still at home. So they bowed down to Joseph, 15 who asked them, "What have you done? Didn't you know I could find out?"

16 "Sir, what can we say?" Judah replied. "How can we prove we are innocent? God has shown that we are guilty. And now all of us are your slaves, especially the one who had the cup."

17 Joseph told them, "I would never punish all of you. Only the one who was caught with the cup will become my slave. The rest of you are free to go home to your father."

CHAPTER 45

1 Since Joseph could no longer control his feelings in front of his servants, he sent them out of the room. When he was alone with his brothers, he told them,

"I am Joseph." 2 Then he cried so loudly that the Egyptians heard him and told about it in the king's palace.

3 Joseph asked his brothers if his father was still alive, but they were too frightened to answer. 4 Joseph told them to come closer to him, and when they did, he said:

Yes, I am your brother Joseph, the one you sold into Egypt. 5 Don't worry or blame yourselves for what you did. God is the one who sent me ahead of you to save lives.

6 There has already been a famine for two years, and for five more years no one will plough fields or harvest grain. 7 But God sent me on ahead of you to keep your families alive and to save you in this wonderful way. 8 After all, you weren't really the ones who sent me here—it was God. He made me the highest official in the king's court and placed me over all Egypt.

9 Now hurry back and tell my father that his son Joseph says, "God has made me ruler of Egypt. Come here as quickly as you can. 10 You will

live near me in the region of Goshen with your children and grandchildren, as well as with your sheep, goats, cattle, and everything else you own. [11] I will take care of you there during the next five years of famine. But if you don't come, you and your family and your animals will starve to death."

[12] All of you, including my brother Benjamin, can tell by what I have said that I really am Joseph. [13] Tell my father about my great power here in Egypt and about everything you have seen. Hurry and bring him here.

[14] Joseph and Benjamin hugged each other and started crying. [15] Joseph was still crying as he kissed each of his other brothers. After this, they started talking with Joseph.

[16] When it was told in the palace that Joseph's brothers had come, the king and his officials were happy. [17] So the king said to Joseph:

Tell your brothers to load their donkeys and return to Canaan. [18] They must bring their father and their families here. I will give them the best land in Egypt, and they can eat and enjoy everything that grows on it.

[19] Also tell your brothers to take some wagons from Egypt for their wives and children to ride in. And they must be sure to bring their father. [20] They can leave their possessions behind, because they will be given the best of everything in Egypt.

[21] Jacob's sons agreed to do what the king had said. And Joseph gave them wagons and food for their trip home, just as the king had ordered. [22] Joseph gave some new clothes to each of his brothers, but to Benjamin he gave five new outfits and three hundred pieces of silver. [23] To his father he sent ten donkeys loaded with the best things in Egypt, and ten other donkeys loaded with grain and bread and other food for the return trip. [24] Then he sent his brothers off and told them, "Don't argue on the way home!"

[25] Joseph's brothers left Egypt, and when they arrived in Canaan, [26] they told their father that Joseph was still alive and was the ruler of Egypt. But their father was so surprised that he could not believe them. [27] Then they told him everything Joseph had said. When he saw the wagons Joseph had sent, he felt

much better [28] and said, "Now I can believe you! My son Joseph must really be alive, and I will get to see him before I die."

CHAPTER 46

[1] Jacob packed up everything he owned and left for Egypt. On the way he stopped near the town of Beersheba and offered sacrifices to the God his father Isaac had worshipped. [2] That night, God spoke to him and said, "Jacob! Jacob!"

"Here I am," Jacob answered.

[3] God said, "I am God, the same God your father worshipped. Don't be afraid to go to Egypt. I will give you so many descendants that one day they will become a nation. [4] I will go with you to Egypt, and later I will bring your descendants back here. Your son Joseph will be at your side when you die."

CHAPTER 50

[15] After Jacob died, Joseph's brothers said to each other, "What if Joseph still

hates us and wants to get even with us for all the cruel things we did to him?"

16 So they sent this message to Joseph:

Before our father died, 17 he told us, "You did some cruel and terrible things to Joseph, but you must ask him to forgive you."

Now we ask you to forgive the terrible things we did. After all, we serve the same God that your father worshipped.

When Joseph heard this, he started crying.

18 At once, Joseph's brothers came and bowed down to the ground in front of him and said, "We are your slaves."

19 But Joseph told them, "Don't be afraid! I have no right to change what God has decided. 20 You tried to harm me, but God made it turn out for the best, so that he could save all these people, as he is now doing. 21 Don't be afraid! I will take care of you and your children." After Joseph said this, his brothers felt much better.

CAN YOU REMEMBER?

Have you learnt the **PYRAMID ROCK** memory verse? You may have learnt it as a song or with the words that are found in the Bible. It was part of a long speech that Stephen, one of the church leaders, made in the first century, just before he was put to death. Stephen realised how important Joseph was in the story of God's people. Work it out using this code.

'Joseph's brothers were jealous of him, and sold him as a slave to be taken to Egypt.

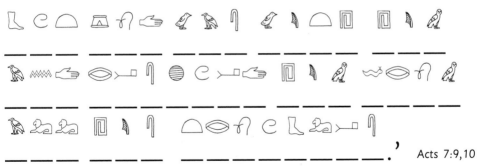

Acts 7:9,10

b c d e f g h i l m n o r s t u/v w y

37

BROTHERS COME TO EGYPT

Joseph's family in Canaan also suffered from the famine. They had to go to Egypt to buy food that their brother, Joseph, had been storing all those years. Look on page 6 to see how far they came.

They did not recognise Joseph, but he recognised them. Joseph wanted to know if his brothers had changed. So he kept his brother Simeon in Egypt until the brothers returned with his youngest brother, Benjamin.

Jacob, his father, did not want Benjamin to leave him. He was still sad because he thought Joseph was dead. But at last, the family was so short of food that the other brothers just had to go back to Egypt and take Benjamin with them. You can read about that in Genesis 43 on pages 28 and 29.

When they had collected their grain, Joseph played a trick on his brothers. He hid his own silver cup in Benjamin's sack of grain and then accused Benjamin of stealing from him. He said Benjamin would be punished. It was then that Judah pleaded with Joseph to be merciful. He said he would be punished instead of Benjamin. Joseph realised that his brothers really had changed.

WHO SAID WHAT?

If you had been Joseph, you might have said this to your brothers when you first met them.

But instead, Joseph said this. Check what he said in Genesis 45:3–8 on page 32.

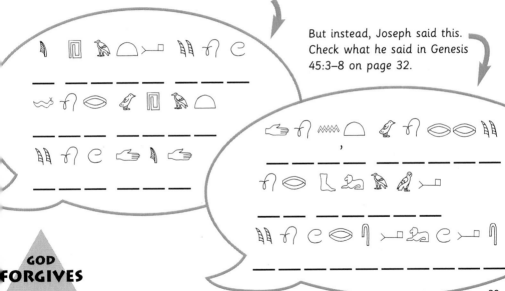

GOD FORGIVES

The codebreaker is on page 37.

39

SPOT THE DIFFERENC

Can you spot ten differences between these two pictures of the brothers?

OSEPH FORGAVE

Joseph was so sure of God's plans that he was able to forgive his brothers. God had planned that Joseph would be able to save people from dying of hunger.

Jesus was also able to forgive the people who put him to death. He loved them. He also knew that his death made it possible for people to know God's forgiveness for the wrong things they've done. That was part of God's big plan. If we know God has forgiven us, God can help us forgive others.

Say this prayer thoughtfully. You may want to talk with a leader about how God can forgive you. You may want to ask God to help you forgive someone in particular.

Dear God,
Thank you that you love me.
Thank you that you can forgive me.
Please help me to forgive others.

A HAPPY ENDING

GOD IS KING

Joseph's brothers went home to break the news to their father. At last, Jacob was going to meet his long-lost son, the one he thought was dead! The whole family set off for Egypt. A long way off, Joseph saw his father coming towards him and raced in his chariot to meet him. He was so happy! Wow! After all these years!

Jacob (who was also known as Israel) and the family settled in Egypt in a place called Goshen. Here they kept their sheep, cattle and goats. Joseph looked after his family well. Read what Joseph said in Genesis 50:15–21 on pages 35 and 36.

Many years later the Egyptians got fed up with the people of Israel and made life very difficult for them in Egypt. You can read about that in the next book of the Bible, Exodus. That is the story of Moses.

OSEPH WRITES TO HIS DAD

Imagine you are Joseph telling your dad you are alive and inviting him to come to Egypt. What will you write? If you like, you can draw a picture instead.

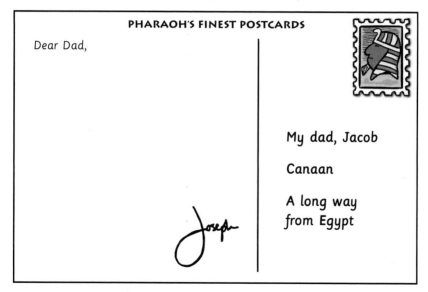

PHARAOH'S FINEST POSTCARDS

Dear Dad,

Joseph

My dad, Jacob

Canaan

A long way from Egypt

43

GOD SPEAKS TO JACOB

Read Genesis 46:1–4 on page 35 and fill in the words that God said to Jacob.

I am _____

I will _____ so many _____

I will _____ with _____ to _____

God is a king and cares for his people. He cares for you too. Make a list of all the things God has done for you or given you.

_____

_____

_____

44 _____

Some of the things that happen to you may seem hard but God loves us. He will take care of us – just as he cared for Joseph.

What does that make you want to say to God?

_____

THE BEST BITS OF PYRAMID ROCK

The funniest bit _____

The most interesting bit _____

The silliest bit _____

The bit I learnt about God _____

The bit I will remember _____

45

SQUIGGLES PAG

Collect the names of your group and leaders!